Quirky

Angie's Patterns - Volume 14

Color With Angie & Friends

Join our friendly Color With Angie Grace Facebook group!

www.AngieGrace.com

Visit Angie's website for special web exclusives for colorists.

Made in the USA
San Bernardino, CA
24 July 2015